Home Sweet *New* Home
Exploring New Construction for Modern Living

By Latosca Lynette Asberry

Home Sweet New Home
By Latosca Lynette Asberry

1st Paperback Edition
ISBN-13: 979-8-218-54418-8

Printed in the United States of America

Acknowledgements
Yolanda Westmorland
Karen Clark
Makeda Smith
Gerogette Jones
James Cianelli
Mesha Miller
Kelly Stone

Introduction

Raised in the outskirts of Dallas and educated at Tarrant County College and Dallas Baptist University, I've cultivated deep roots within the community. My genuine passion lies in helping individuals and families discover their perfect homes—spaces where they can build their dreams and futures.

I believe in empowering people with knowledge to make informed decisions. For many, owning a home is a cherished lifelong dream, yet the process can often feel overwhelming and complex. With abundant information circulating on social media and within communities, it's challenging for buyers to discern whom to trust and where to begin their journey.

My mission is to bridge that gap for you. I've drawn from all my available resources to craft this comprehensive guide, providing an authentic roadmap for your home buying journey. Even if you choose not to use my services, you'll have the knowledge to navigate this process with confidence.

A new construction home is more than just a place to live; it's an opportunity to lay the foundation for your future and design a sanctuary where you and your family can thrive. My goal is to ensure that your new construction journey is successful but also fulfilling and rewarding.

Join me as your guide through the pages of this book, where I share my expertise and insights on every step of purchasing a new construction home. From understanding the advantages of new builds to navigating financing options, selecting the right builder, customizing your home, and managing the construction timeline, you'll be equipped with the information necessary to make decisions that reflect your style and needs.

As a real estate agent specializing in new construction homes in the Dallas Fort Worth area, I bring a decade of experience in banking, retail sales, and medical. With an in-depth understanding of the real estate market and the new construction process, I'm here to empower you with valuable advice.

Let's start on this exciting journey into the world of new construction homes together, paving the way for your next chapter. Prepare to make informed decisions as you purchase the perfect new construction home tailored to your desires!

Chapter 1: The Importance of Having a Real Estate Agent

The role of a real estate agent is valuable in the process of buying or selling a property, as they bring expertise, guidance, and support to navigate the complexities of the real estate market. From their knowledge of market trends and negotiation skills to their ability to streamline the buying or selling process, a real estate agent ensures a successful and smooth transaction. By understanding the importance of having a real estate agent, you can make informed decisions leading to a positive experience.

A real estate agent specializing in new construction homes offers a wealth of knowledge and guidance. They are knowledgeable about navigating the home buying process and provide valuable insights into contract terms, builder policies, and potential pitfalls, ensuring you start your home buying journey with clarity and confidence.

Signs of an Experienced Real Estate Agent
- They should be familiar with the major builders in the area, their reputations, and the quality of their work
- They should be able to explain the construction process, ie timelines, what to expect at each stage, etc.
- They should know the options for upgrades and customizations available from different builders and how these affect pricing

- They should be well-versed in the specifics of new construction contracts, including builder warranties and contingencies
- They should understand the financing options for new construction homes, including any incentives offered by builders' preferred lenders

Questions to Ask a Real Estate Agent

- Can you provide information about the major builders in this area and their reputations?
- Have you worked with this particular builder before? What was your experience?
- Can you explain the typical construction process and timeline for a new construction home?
- What options do I have for upgrades and customizations with this builder?
- What kind of warranties does the builder provide on the home?
- Do I need to be pre-approved through the builder's lender even if I plan to use my own lender?
- Are there any incentives for using the builder's preferred lender?
- Will I still need an independent inspection if the builder conducts several inspections throughout the process?
- Can you recommend a reputable inspector who specializes in new construction?
- What are the current market conditions for new construction homes in this area?
- Are there any future developments planned that could impact property values or the quality of life in this community?

- Are there any Homeowner's Association (HOA) fees or rules I should know in this community?
- Can I change my mind in the middle of this real estate transaction? If so, how long do I have?

Real estate agents have established relationships with local builders, granting them access to insider information on available homes, upcoming projects, and builder incentives. Leveraging these connections, agents can negotiate on your behalf and uncover promotions, discounts, and benefits that align with your preferences and budget.

Armed with negotiation skills, a real estate agent advocates for your interests in dealings with the builder. They skillfully navigate price negotiations and upgrades, ensuring your needs and desires are safeguarded throughout the negotiation process.

Real estate agents understand the local market, offering insights into comparable sales, market trends, and property values. Their market understanding allows you to make informed decisions, secure fair pricing, and confidently navigate the complexities of the new construction home market.

While new construction homes undergo detailed inspections, having a real estate agent by your side provides additional protection. They recommend independent home inspectors, review inspection reports, and ensure the home meets your expectations and complies with building codes, offering peace of mind and assurance.

Entrusting the guidance of a trusted real estate professional throughout the new construction home buying journey instills peace of mind and confidence. Their expertise, advocacy, and unwavering support help navigate challenges, streamline the process, and alleviate stress, allowing you to focus on the excitement of homeownership.

It's noteworthy that builder contracts often include provisions for agent representation, with the builder typically covering the professional fee for the buyer's agent. Therefore, enlisting the services of a real estate agent comes at no extra cost to you as the buyer, making their expertise and support a valuable asset in your home buying journey.

In essence, a real estate agent is instrumental in the new construction home buying process, offering knowledge, advocacy, and support to empower you in making sound decisions and safeguarding your interests every step of the way. Their expertise and guidance pave the way for a seamless and rewarding home buying experience, ensuring you start your homeownership journey with confidence, clarity, and peace of mind.

If you're considering purchasing a new construction home, working with a real estate agent who specializes in this area is important. A knowledgeable agent can guide you through the new construction process and help you make informed decisions.

I can help you find an agent with expertise in new construction. With an extensive network of real estate agents, I can connect you with a professional who understands new construction details and can help you find the perfect home tailored to your preferences. Your satisfaction and peace of mind are my top priorities, and I'm here to support you every step of the way in your home buying journey. My contact information is at the end of this book.

Brokerage Services and the Buyer Representation Agreement[1]

When finding your dream home, it's paramount to understand the various roles, responsibilities, and agreements involved in working with real estate professionals. Two key documents that will shape your home buying experience are the Information About Brokerage Services (IABS) and the Buyer Representation Agreement.

The Information About Brokerage Services (IABS) document states that real estate agents must provide information to potential buyers, sellers, tenants, and landlords. Its primary purpose is to ensure that you, as a client, are fully informed about the types of brokerage services available, the duties and obligations of a real estate agent.

A Buyer Representation Agreement is a formal contract between you, the buyer, and a real estate agent or brokerage. This agreement outlines the terms of the relationship, including the duties and obligations of both parties. It is designed to protect both the buyer and the agent, ensuring a clear understanding of expectations.

Understanding the Information About Brokerage Services (IABS) and the Buyer Representation Agreement is necessary to navigate the real estate market. These documents clarify, establish trust, and ensure that you and your agent are on the same page. By familiarizing yourself with these agreements, you'll be better prepared to make informed decisions and move one step closer to finding your new home.

---

[1] https://www.nar.realtor/the-facts/written-buyer-agreements-101

"It's important to note that some new homes may not come equipped with certain essential items, such as refrigerators and blinds, etc. Be sure to clarify with the builder what is included in the purchase to avoid any surprises and plan accordingly for additional purchases."

If you are currently under contract with another real estate agent, you must direct all your questions and communications to your designated realtor. Consulting with multiple realtors while under contract can lead to conflicts of interest and potential breaches of your existing agreement.

It is important to disclose if you are working with another realtor to avoid potential issues. This transparency ensures ethical practices and maintains professional integrity.

How to Terminate a Real Estate Agent

Having the right real estate agent by your side can make a huge difference in the home buying process. However, there may come a time when you find it necessary to terminate your relationship with your agent. This could be due to various reasons, such as poor performance, communication issues, or simply not feeling like the agent is the right fit for your needs. Here's how to do this professionally.

Understanding your agreement is crucial. Start by reviewing the duration, exclusivity, and cancellation clauses in your buyer's agency agreement, and make sure you are aware of any penalties for early termination. When you decide to communicate your decision, choose a method that suits your comfort level—an in-person meeting or a phone call. Email is also a professional and acceptable way to convey your decision. Regardless of the method you choose, it's important to follow up with a formal written notice. As you proceed, keep in mind the legal and ethical considerations. Adhere to all contract terms outlined in your agreement, and seek legal advice if necessary. Throughout the process, handle the termination with honesty and professionalism.

Below is a sample termination script you can use for any written notice:

Hi [Agent's Name], I appreciate your efforts, but after careful consideration, I've decided to terminate our agreement effective [date]. I believe it's best for me to explore other options. Thank you for understanding.

Terminating a real estate agent should be done thoughtfully and professionally. You can ensure a smooth transition by understanding your agreement and communicating clearly.

Chapter 1 has highlighted the role of a real estate agent in your home buying journey, especially when navigating the complexities of the new construction market. Real estate agents provide valuable expertise, guidance, and support, ensuring a smooth and successful process whether you're buying or selling. Their deep understanding of market trends, negotiation skills, and ability to streamline transactions are instrumental in achieving the best outcomes for your real estate endeavors. A specialized real estate agent offers even more tailored support for those considering new construction homes. They are adept at dealing with builders, understanding contract terms, and identifying potential pitfalls, all essential for a seamless home buying experience. By asking the right questions and leveraging established relationships with builders, agents can negotiate favorable terms and uncover valuable incentives that align with your budget and preferences.

Additionally, real estate agents provide peace of mind by recommending independent inspections, reviewing reports, and ensuring compliance with building codes, further safeguarding your investment. Their services, often covered by the builder, come at no additional cost to you, making their expertise a vital resource on your journey. As you start on the path to homeownership, understanding the importance of brokerage services and the Buyer Representation Agreement is important. These documents lay the groundwork for a transparent and effective partnership with your agent, ensuring all parties are aligned in their goals and expectations. In summary, partnering with a knowledgeable real estate agent empowers you to make informed decisions, protect your interests, and enjoy a rewarding experience. Whether you're exploring new construction or other real estate opportunities, their expertise paves the way for a confident and successful journey into homeownership.

Chapter 2: Choosing Your Community

When selecting a new construction home, you're investing not only in a house but also in a community. By exploring various community types, amenities, and school ratings, you gain valuable insights into the factors that shape the lifestyle and environment of a community. Recognizing the importance of these elements is crucial to making an informed decision that aligns with your preferences, needs, and aspirations.

Community Types and Their Locations

When considering new communities, several common types offer distinct lifestyles and locations. Suburban developments are typically found on the outskirts of major cities or towns, providing neighborhoods with single-family homes and amenities like parks, schools, and shopping centers. They are ideal for families seeking more space and a quieter environment. Infill development communities within city limits often use previously underutilized or industrial areas. These areas offer residential and mixed-use options, attracting buyers who desire proximity to city amenities and a walkable lifestyle. Master-planned communities can be found in suburban and rural areas, offering large-scale developments with residential, commercial, and recreational spaces, often complemented by golf courses, pools, and community centers. These cater to individuals seeking a comprehensive living environment. Active adult or retirement communities are usually situated in warmer climates or scenic areas, although they can be found nationwide. Designed for those aged 55 and over, these communities provide maintenance-free living, social activities, and amenities like golf courses and fitness centers, appealing to retirees and those pursuing an active lifestyle. Additionally, boutique communities are emerging in various locations, often in urban or desirable suburban areas. These smaller, more exclusive developments focus on unique architecture and personalized living experiences, attracting buyers looking for distinct character and a sense of community.

Amenities

In the essence of neighborhood living, community amenities serve as the threads that weave shared experiences, opportunities, and connections. Designed to elevate quality of life and foster a sense of belonging, these conveniences offer many opportunities for recreation, relaxation, and social engagement within their community. From fitness centers to parks, pools to playgrounds, community amenities shape the fabric of community life. Here are some common examples of community amenities that enrich the residential experience and contribute to the dynamic atmosphere of neighborhood living:

The clubhouse is a versatile space that serves as a hub of activity. It offers residents a range of amenities such as fitness centers, meeting rooms, lounges, and sometimes even swimming pools or other sports facilities. It is a gathering place for social events.

Parks and Green Spaces: Retreats within the community—parks and green spaces—offer residents a serene backdrop for outdoor activities, picnics, and strolls. These areas encourage outdoor enjoyment and connection with nature, featuring playgrounds, walking trails, picnic areas, and designated dog parks.

Community Events and Programs: Fostering a social fabric, community events and programs such as holiday parties, movie nights, fitness classes, and workshops create opportunities for residents to connect, celebrate, and learn, nurturing community spirit and togetherness.

Lake: A community with a lake offers opportunities for recreational activities such as fishing, boating, kayaking, and paddleboarding. The serene and picturesque setting of a lake provides a peaceful escape and a natural gathering spot to relax, socialize, and enjoy the beauty of the outdoors. Residents can also take advantage of walking or biking trails around the lake, creating a scenic and active lifestyle within the community.

Duck Pond: A duck pond adds charm and character to a community, creating a tranquil and inviting atmosphere for residents to enjoy. Watching ducks and other wildlife in the pond can be a soothing and enjoyable experience, connecting residents with nature and providing a sense of serenity. The presence of a duck pond can also attract birdwatchers and nature enthusiasts, fostering a sense of environmental stewardship and appreciation for the local ecosystem.

Beach: A community with a beach area offers residents a place to relax, sunbathe, swim, and engage in water activities without traveling far from home. The beach can serve as a social hub for gatherings, picnics, and events, fostering a sense of community and belonging among residents. Additionally, amenities such as beach volleyball courts, playgrounds, and picnic areas can enhance the recreational opportunities and lifestyle options available within the community.

School Ratings

As families begin relocating to a new community, the quality of education and school ratings are pivotal considerations in shaping the future and well-being of their children. School ratings in new communities vary based on the location, school district, and academic performance, highlighting the importance of thorough research and informed decision-making. Here are key points to consider when exploring school ratings in new communities:

School performance rankings provide valuable insights into the academic excellence and success of schools within a district. These rankings are often based on criteria such as standardized test scores, graduation rates, teacher qualifications, and student-to-teacher ratios. Platforms like Great Schools, Niche[2], and state education department websites offer comprehensive school ratings and rankings to aid your evaluation.

For a firsthand perspective on the educational environment, consider visiting schools in the new community and engaging with administrators, educators, and parents. This in-depth experience allows you to assess school facilities, academic programs, extracurricular offerings, and the school's overall culture. Conversations with parents whose children attend the school can provide valuable insights into their experiences and perspectives.

Real estate professionals in the local area can offer valuable guidance on school ratings and educational opportunities in

---

[2] https://www.niche.com/

the new community. Leveraging their expertise, insights, and resources can facilitate your research process and help you navigate the complexities of evaluating school options.

Recognize that school ratings are just one aspect of the broader educational landscape in a new community. Personal preferences, family needs, extracurricular offerings, special programs, and support services should also be factored into your decision-making process to ensure a holistic evaluation of educational opportunities that align with your children's academic, social, and developmental needs. By conducting thorough research, engaging with the school community, and seeking professional advice, you can make informed choices that prioritize your children's educational growth and success in the new community.

Chapter 3: Designing Your Perfect Home

Working with Latosca was a game-changer in our home buying experience. Her deep knowledge of the real estate market and the new construction process helped us make informed decisions every step of the way. From selecting the right builder to customizing our dream home, Latosca's attention to detail and dedication ensured we found the perfect home for our family. Her professionalism, personalized approach, and commitment to our satisfaction truly set her apart. We couldn't be happier with our new home and owe it all to Latosca's expertise.
-Lewis Jackson

Standard Features

In new construction homes, standard features define the aesthetic and functionality of the design. These features, included in the base price of the home, offer a glimpse into the craftsmanship, quality, and style that homeowners can expect. While the specifics of standard features may vary depending on the builder and price range, here are some common elements typically included in new construction homes:

Flooring

By understanding the qualities of vinyl, laminate, and wood flooring options, homeowners can select the best flooring type that aligns with their style preferences, lifestyle needs, and budget considerations for their new construction home.

Vinyl flooring is a versatile and popular cost-effective option. Available in various designs, including wood, tile, and stone patterns, vinyl flooring offers the look of natural materials with added benefits. Vinyl is known for its water resistance, making it ideal for high-moisture areas like kitchens and bathrooms. It is also durable, easy to clean, and comfortable underfoot. With advancements in technology, vinyl flooring can replicate the look and texture of natural materials while providing added resilience and low maintenance requirements.

Laminate flooring is a practical and affordable choice. It consists of multiple layers fused through a lamination process, creating a durable and versatile flooring option. Laminate flooring can mimic the appearance of hardwood, tile, or stone, offering a wide range of design options. It is known for its scratch and stain resistance, making it suitable for active households with pets or children. Easy installation and low maintenance requirements make laminate flooring a popular choice for those seeking a balance of style and functionality.

Wood flooring is a timeless and luxurious option that adds warmth and elegance to new construction homes. This flooring choice offers natural beauty, durability, and longevity, whether for solid hardwood or engineered wood. Hardwood flooring comes in various species, finishes, and plank sizes, allowing homeowners to customize their floors to complement their design preferences. Wood flooring ages gracefully, developing a unique finish over time, and can be refinished to restore its original beauty. While hardwood flooring may require more maintenance than vinyl or laminate, its enduring appeal and value make it a sought after choice for homeowners looking to invest in quality flooring.

Countertops

Countertops in kitchens and bathrooms serve as usable workspaces and design focal points. Standard countertops, which may vary in material and finish, often feature options like laminate, granite, or quartz, offering a blend of practicality and aesthetic appeal.

Granite countertops are renowned for their natural beauty, durability, and timeless appeal. Harvested from the earth, granite slabs exhibit unique patterns, colors, and textures that add a touch of luxury and elegance to any kitchen or bathroom. Beyond their aesthetic charm, granite countertops are incredibly durable and heat-resistant, making them ideal for high-traffic areas and culinary spaces. The natural stone surface of granite is also easy to clean and maintain, ensuring long-lasting beauty and functionality. Homeowners are often drawn to granite countertops for their distinctive appearance, durability, and investment value as they can enhance a home's overall aesthetic and resale potential.

Quartz countertops offer a perfect blend of beauty and practicality, making them a popular choice for new construction homes. Engineered from natural quartz crystals and polymers, quartz countertops provide a durable, non-absorbent surface resistant to stains, scratches, and heat. Available in a wide range of colors, patterns, and finishes, quartz countertops offer versatility to suit various design styles and preferences. Homeowners are drawn to quartz for its low maintenance requirements, hygienic properties, and consistency in color and pattern. The durability and longevity of quartz countertops make them a reliable and stylish choice for those seeking a balance of aesthetics and functionality in their living spaces.

Homeowners can create a sense of luxury, style, and elegance beyond mere functionality by incorporating laminate, granite, or quartz countertops in a new construction home. These countertop materials enhance a home's visual appeal and provide lasting value, durability, and sophistication that can truly impress and elevate the living experience to new heights.

Cabinetry

Cabinetry, an element of the kitchen and bathroom design, provides essential storage and organization solutions. Standard cabinets are crafted from wood or wood composite and may feature painted or stained finishes.

Appliances

Appliances bring convenience and efficiency to daily living routines. Stainless steel stoves, ovens, dishwashers, and microwaves from reputable brands enhance both functionality and style in the home.

Light Fixtures

Light fixtures brighten living spaces and contribute to the home's overall mood. Overhead lighting in each room, complemented by decorative fixtures such as chandeliers or pendant lights in select areas, fosters a welcoming and well-lit atmosphere for everyday activities.

Paint

Interior paint selections set the tone for the home's overall color palette. Typically chosen in a neutral shade, standard paint creates a versatile backdrop that allows homeowners to personalize and enhance the space with their preferred hues and accents.

Smart Technology Packages

A smart home is equipped with various technologies and devices that enhance convenience, efficiency, security, and comfort for homeowners. What sets a smart home apart is its integration of systems that can be controlled remotely or automated to perform tasks, monitor surroundings, and optimize energy usage.

Smart homes feature automation systems that allow homeowners to control lighting, heating, cooling, appliances, and security systems from a central device or smartphone. This level of automation provides convenience and options to adapt the home environment to individual preferences.

Voice Control

Voice-activated assistants, such as Amazon Alexa, Google Assistant, or Apple Siri, are commonly integrated into smart homes. These assistants allow users to control devices, play music, set reminders, and access information through voice commands. This hands-free functionality adds another layer of convenience and accessibility to smart home technology.

Elevation Styles

Elevation styles play a crucial role in determining a newly constructed home's aesthetic appeal and character. They range from traditional and timeless designs to modern and sleek architecture, and the choice of elevation style sets the tone for the entire exterior look. Each elevation style has unique features and influences that reflect different architectural traditions, periods, and inspirations. Whether you prefer the classic charm of a Craftsman-style home, the clean lines of a contemporary design, or the rustic elegance of a farmhouse aesthetic, understanding elevation styles can help you envision the look and feel of your dream home. Here are some common types of elevations that showcase a variety of designs and aesthetic features:

Traditional Elevation

Embracing classic architectural styles like Colonial, Victorian, or Craftsman, traditional elevations radiate timeless elegance and sophistication. They are characterized by balanced designs, detailed features, and traditional materials such as brick, stone, or wood and pay homage to historical design elements and craftsmanship.

Modern or Contemporary Elevation

Defined by clean lines, minimalist decoration, and a focus on simplicity and functionality, modern or contemporary elevations embrace a sleek and sophisticated design approach. These elevations showcase modern elegance and innovation, including expansive windows, open layouts, and sleek materials like glass, steel, and concrete.

Farmhouse Elevation

Drawing inspiration from rustic and rural aesthetics, Farmhouse elevations radiate a cozy and inviting charm. Farmhouse elevations capture the essence of country living and timeless appeal with gable roofs, horizontal siding, expansive porches, and understated yet elegant details.

Tudor Elevation

Inspired by Tudor-era architecture, Tudor elevations showcase distinctive timber-framed exteriors, steeply pitched roofs, decorative half-timbering, and masonry or stone accents. Evoking a sense of old-world charm and architectural heritage, Tudor elevations exude a timeless and elegant appeal.

These examples offer a glimpse into the rich variety of elevation styles available in home design, each with unique appeal and character. When selecting an elevation for your home, consider your personal preferences, the architectural context of your surroundings, and the overall design narrative you wish to convey. Choosing an elevation that resonates with your vision and lifestyle allows you to create a harmonious and visually captivating living space that reflects your individuality and design sensibilities.

The Design Center & Upgrades

The design center is a hub of creativity for new construction homes, allowing buyers to tailor their living spaces to reflect their unique style and preferences. This chapter reviews the importance of the design center and the process of selecting upgrades to create a home that aligns with your vision and lifestyle.

As a sanctuary of inspiration and choice, the design center allows buyers to start a transformative journey of selecting and customizing various features, finishes, and upgrades for their new homes. From flooring and cabinetry to countertops, appliances, fixtures, and paint colors, the design center presents a wealth of possibilities for buyers to infuse their personal touch into every aspect of their new home.

Guided by design consultants, buyers navigate the selection process through scheduled appointments at the design center. These experts present available options, explain features and functionalities, and assist buyers in curating finishes that align with their preferences and budgets.

Beyond the standard features included in the base price of the home, the design center encourages buyers to explore upgrades ranging from subtle enhancements to transformative modifications. Whether upgrading to premium appliances, adding extra rooms, or opting for luxurious finishes, the design center offers a canvas for buyers to elevate their living space to new levels of elegance and comfort.

Upgrades come with additional costs, depending on the complexity, materials, and options chosen. Buyers are advised to carefully evaluate these costs and integrate them thoughtfully into their overall budget, achieving a balance between desired enhancements and financial feasibility.

Operating within the builder's guidelines, the design center provides a curated selection of options to maintain consistency and quality standards. While some builders may allow flexibility for customizations beyond standard choices, the feasibility of such requests may vary based on the construction stage and complexity.

The design center process unfolds within designated stages of the construction timeline, requiring buyers to be mindful of selection deadlines. Adhering to these timelines ensures a smooth construction process and helps bring the envisioned home design to life on time.

Personalization and enhancement through specific customization options or upgrades can significantly elevate the value of your new construction home. These enhancements can increase the property's market worth, amplifying your equity and strengthening your investment. However, it is important to avoid overvaluing your home by investing more than its market value.

To streamline the customization journey, some builders offer online tools or catalogs for buyers to explore options and make preliminary selections before their design center appointments. These resources allow buyers to familiarize themselves with available choices and refine their preferences, approaching the design center experience with clarity and confidence.

Effective communication with design center professionals, transparency about preferences, budget constraints, and timeline considerations are crucial for a successful customization experience. By collaborating closely with the builder and design center team, buyers can navigate the details of upgrades, unleash their creativity, and craft a home that embodies their aspirations, style, and functional needs, resulting in a living space that truly reflects their dreams and desires.

Designing your perfect home underscores the importance of considering aspects such as standard features, elevation styles, and the design center in the home design process. By focusing on these elements, you can create a home that reflects your individuality, enhances your daily living experience, and incorporates the latest advancements in technology for added convenience and efficiency. Embracing these key components lays the foundation for a space that is not only beautiful and well-crafted but also tailored to your specific needs and preferences, ultimately resulting in a home that truly feels like a reflection of you.

Chapter 4: Building Basics

B uilding a new construction home is an exciting and transformative experience. However, it's also a process filled with critical decisions and detailed planning. Each step is crucial for ensuring a smooth and successful outcome, from selecting the right builder to understanding the costs involved, navigating the construction timeline, and managing your living arrangements during the build. This chapter aims to provide a comprehensive overview of these aspects, equipping you with the knowledge and confidence needed to make informed decisions throughout your new home construction journey.

Types of Builders

In the ever-evolving world of new construction homes, builders represent a diverse blend of expertise, innovation, and craftsmanship. Understanding the different types of builders can provide valuable insights into the construction process and help prospective homebuyers make informed decisions. Here are some common types of builders you may encounter in the industry:

Spec Builders

Spec builders, also known as speculative builders or inventory builders, begin constructing homes without a designated buyer in mind. These builders observe market trends and preferences to craft homes that appeal to potential buyers. Spec homes are often infused with popular features and finishes strategically designed to attract interested buyers seeking a move-in ready solution.

Production Builders

Production builders operate on efficiency and scale, constructing homes based on pre-designed floor plans within larger developments or communities. These builders offer a range of home models and floor plans, allowing for some customization options within established parameters. Focusing on delivering quality homes at a competitive price point, production builders streamline the construction process to meet the demands of a broader market.

Luxury Home Builders

Luxury home builders represent elegance and sophistication. They specialize in crafting high-end, custom-designed homes with premium features and finishes. These builders cater to buyers seeking unparalleled craftsmanship, exclusive materials, and architectural excellence. Collaborating with renowned architects and designers, luxury home builders create exceptional homes that radiate opulence and distinction.

Custom Home Builders

Custom home builders represent personalized craftsmanship, specializing in creating custom homes tailored to the unique needs and desires of the homeowner. Collaborating closely with buyers, these builders translate individual visions into reality, infusing each home with distinctive features and personalized touches. Custom home builders prioritize attention to detail and customization to guarantee each home reflects the homeowner's lifestyle and aesthetic.

The Cost

Purchasing a new home is an exciting venture, but understanding the full scope of the costs involved is important for making an informed decision. This chapter covers the financial aspects associated with buying a new home.

The Base Price

The base price of a new construction home represents the starting point of your financial investment. This price typically includes the standard home model with basic features and finishes specified by the builder.

The Contract Price

The contract price is the final agreed-upon price between you and the builder. This includes the base price plus the costs of any upgrades, customization, and additional fees.

Negotiating the Contract Price

Understanding what is included in the contract price and what can be negotiated is key. Some builders may offer incentives or discounts, particularly if they are eager to sell the last few homes in a development or if you are willing to close quickly.

Standard and Premium Lots

Standard lots are typically the default option offered by builders. They are usually smaller and have fewer desirable features compared to premium lots.

Premium lots offer additional features or advantages, such as larger size, better views, or more privacy. They are often located in more desirable parts of the community and cost more.

Supplementary Costs

Upgrades and Enhancements
While the base price covers standard features and finishes, many homeowners opt for upgrades to enhance their homes. These upgrades can include:
- High-end Appliances
- Premium Flooring
- Custom Cabinetry

Building a new construction home is a significant financial undertaking. Still, with careful planning and a thorough understanding of the costs, you can make informed decisions that align with your budget and lifestyle. By considering the base price, contract price, lot options, and supplementary costs, you'll be well-equipped to embark on your new home journey with confidence.

The Timeline

Building a new home is a thrilling journey filled with anticipation and excitement. Understanding the timeline and phases of the construction process can help you navigate each step with confidence. Here, you'll find an outline of the stages from initial planning to move-in day, providing a clear roadmap to your dream home.

Phase 1: Pre-Construction Planning (Month 1)
- Discuss your vision, budget, and desired timeline with the builder
- Review and select floor plans, elevation styles, and customization features
- Choose and purchase a suitable lot for your new home
- Finalize home design, including floor plans and elevations
- Select interior finishes, smart home technology, and other personalized details

Phase 2: Groundwork and Foundation (Month 2)
- Clear and level the lot in preparation for foundation work
- Excavate, pour footings, and erect foundation walls
- Allow the foundation to cure properly before proceeding

Phase 3: Framing the Structure (Month 3)
- Build the home's frame, including walls, floors, and roof
- Install windows, exterior doors, and roofing materials

Phase 4: Systems and Exterior Details (Months 4-5)
- Install essential systems: electrical wiring, plumbing, and HVAC
- Undergo initial inspections to ensure code compliance
- Apply siding, stonework, or brickwork as per the chosen design

- Paint exterior trim and install roofing details like gutters

Phase 5: Interior Craftsmanship (Months 5-7)
- Insulate walls and ceilings, then hang and finish drywall
- Apply interior paint and install doors, trim, and moldings
- Lay down flooring and install cabinetry and countertops
- Fit out electrical fixtures, faucets, and appliances

Phase 6: Final Details and Inspection (Months 7-8)
- Install hardware for cabinets and doors
- Complete landscaping and any exterior features like driveways or patios
- Conduct final inspections to obtain the certificate of occupancy
- Walk through with the builder for quality assurance and to address any final adjustments

Phase 7: The Big Move (Month 9)
- Confirm move-in dates and coordinate utility transfers
- Move into your newly constructed home and begin your new chapter
-

The journey from groundbreaking to move-in day is a carefully coordinated dance of planning and execution. This timeline allows buyers to navigate the construction process, fully prepared for the exciting journey to their dream home.

Living Arrangements

In the exhilarating journey of building a new home, transitioning from your current residence to the future dwelling under construction requires thoughtful consideration of temporary living arrangements. When deliberating on the optimal living arrangement during the construction phase, factors such as budget constraints, personal preferences, and the anticipated duration of temporary housing merit careful contemplation. Planning and securing temporary accommodations well in advance can streamline the transition process for a stress-free experience as you navigate the interim period before stepping into your new abode.

Renting

Embracing the appeal of flexibility and convenience, renting a house, apartment, or condominium during construction is a popular choice. This option grants you the freedom to inhabit a space without commitment, providing a seamless transition as you await the completion of your new home.

Staying with Family or Friends

For those seeking a blend of familiarity and comfort, staying with family or friends residing nearby presents a welcoming sanctuary during the transition period. Nestling into a familiar environment can offer solace and companionship as you begin the journey into your new home.

Short Term Rentals

Harnessing short-term rental platforms like Airbnb or VRBO unveils diverse lodging options, ranging from apartments to houses and cozy rooms in various locations. This avenue provides choices, allowing you to tailor your temporary living arrangements to your preferences.

Begin this temporary phase with an open mind and a sense of adventure, embracing the opportunities to explore new living spaces, nurture connections with loved ones, and savor the anticipation of settling into your dream home. By selecting a temporary living arrangement that aligns with your needs and aspirations, you can infuse this period with comfort, convenience, and excitement, setting the stage for a smooth and fulfilling transition into your future home.

Building a new construction home is a multifaceted journey that requires careful consideration and planning. By understanding the different types of builders, accurately estimating the costs, familiarizing yourself with the construction timeline, and making informed decisions about your living arrangements during the build, you can navigate this process with greater ease and confidence. This chapter has provided the foundational knowledge to approach each step thoughtfully and strategically. As you move forward, remember that thorough preparation and informed choices are key to turning your dream home into a reality. With the proper guidance and resources, you'll be well on your way to enjoying the rewards of your new construction home.

Chapter 5: Protecting Your Investment

The next step in safeguarding and enhancing the value of your real estate investment involves a deep dive into several key considerations. By examining builder warranties, homeowners associations (HOAs), home inspections, and homeowner's insurance—especially within new communities—you equip yourself with the knowledge necessary to protect your investment and ensure a rewarding homeownership experience. Furthermore, understanding these elements will help you navigate potential challenges and make informed decisions throughout your homeownership journey.. Each aspect plays a crucial role in safeguarding your investment and ensuring that you make informed choices that align with your long-term goals. By exploring the importance of these components, you can gain valuable insights into how to protect and maximize the value of your home investment.

Builder Warranties

When purchasing a new construction home, warranties protect your investment and ensure peace of mind. These warranties typically cover various aspects of your new home, from basic workmanship to structural elements. They can be divided into different categories based on the duration and scope of coverage.

One-Year Warranty

The one-year warranty is the foundation of builder warranties, offering protection for the first year following the closing date or occupancy. This warranty primarily covers workmanship and materials, addressing common issues such as poor craftsmanship, defects in materials, and problems related to the fit and finish of the home. This includes aspects like paint, trim, and fixtures. The purpose of the one-year warranty is to confirm that the basic elements of your home are constructed correctly and meet the agreed-upon standards.

Two-Year Warranty

The two-year warranty typically extends coverage to major systems within the home, such as plumbing, electrical, and HVAC (heating, ventilation, and air conditioning) systems. This warranty ensures that these critical components function properly and meet quality standards. While issues with these systems can be less frequent, their resolution can be more complex and costly, making this warranty particularly valuable.

Ten-Year Structural Warranty

The ten-year structural warranty offers long-term protection for the structure of the home. This warranty covers the foundation, load-bearing walls, beams, and roof framing. Structural defects can be rare but potentially devastating, so having this warranty ensures that the builder addresses any significant issues that arise within the first ten years.

Manufacturer Warranties

In addition to builder warranties, many of the products and appliances installed in your new home come with their own manufacturer warranties. These can include warranties for kitchen appliances, HVAC units, roofing materials, windows, and more. It's important to review these warranties separately to understand their coverage, duration, and any maintenance requirements that must be met to keep them valid.

Familiarizing yourself with the terms and conditions of each warranty is essential. Keep a record of all warranty documents and note the expiration dates. Understanding what is covered, the process for making a claim, and any homeowner maintenance responsibilities can save you time and stress if issues arise.

Warranties for new construction homes provide a safety net that ensures your new home is built to quality standards and that any issues are promptly addressed. By understanding and utilizing these warranties, you can protect your investment and enjoy your new home with greater confidence and peace of mind.

Homeowners Association

In community living, a Homeowners Association (HOA) often serves as a guiding force that shapes the landscape of shared spaces, amenities, and communal responsibilities within a neighborhood. HOAs are a standard fixture in many new communities, playing a vital role in fostering unity and ensuring the upkeep of common areas. Here are key insights into the dynamics of HOAs in new communities:

At the heart of every Homeowners Association (HOA) is a core mission to preserve and elevate the shared spaces and amenities within the community, maintaining a standard of excellence and functionality. From maintaining landscaping and community facilities to overseeing road maintenance and enforcing community regulations, the primary purpose of an HOA is to nurture a thriving, well-maintained living environment for all residents.

Membership in the HOA is typically mandatory within the community, and homeowners are obligated to pay regular dues. These financial contributions serve as the community's foundation, funding ongoing maintenance, repairs, and management activities that uphold the community's quality of life and aesthetic appeal.

HOAs act as custodians of community harmony by establishing and enforcing rules and regulations that govern property usage and appearance within the neighborhood. These guidelines include architectural standards, property maintenance requirements, noise ordinances, and pet policies. Familiarizing yourself with these regulations is crucial if you consider purchasing in an HOA community. Once you commit to a realtor, they can further instruct you on how to get the information you'll need to make a decision. HOAs manage and maintain community amenities like swimming pools, parks, fitness centers, and recreational areas. These amenities not only enrich residents' lifestyles but also contribute to the overall desirability and appeal of the community.

The HOA is responsible for the financial stewardship of the community. It oversees the collection of dues, the development of budgets, and the strategic allocation of funds for ongoing maintenance, repairs, and future enhancements.

Sound financial management ensures the longevity and sustainability of the community's infrastructure and facilities. HOAs operate under the guidance of a board of directors or a governing body composed of elected homeowners. This leadership entity is instrumental in making decisions on behalf of the community, from approving architectural modifications and establishing community guidelines to spearheading community initiatives and projects.

While HOAs offer numerous advantages, such as preserving property values, upholding community standards, and granting access to shared amenities, it's important to weigh the potential limitations, restrictions, and additional costs associated with residing in an HOA community. Understanding the benefits and considerations can empower homeowners to make informed decisions that align with their lifestyle preferences and financial objectives.

As prospective homeowners explore new communities with an HOA presence, examining the association's governing documents, financial reports, and operational procedures can provide valuable insights into the association's structure, rules, and economic health. Engaging with current residents and seeking guidance from real estate professionals who are well-versed in the community can provide a deeper understanding of the HOA's management practices and their impact on the community's dynamics and residents' experiences. By navigating the landscape of HOAs with knowledge, you'll be able to find community living that aligns with your values, expectations, and aspirations for a fulfilling homeownership journey.

When purchasing a home in a community governed by an HOA, it is imperative to highlight the importance of requesting and reviewing the association's declarations before proceeding with the contracting process. These declarations outline the rules, regulations, covenants, and restrictions that must be followed within the community. By obtaining and thoroughly examining the declarations upfront, you will gain a comprehensive understanding of the community's guidelines, fees, amenities, and any restrictions that may impact your lifestyle or property. Being proactive will ensure a smooth transition into the community without any surprises or conflicts.

Home Inspections

Beginning the journey of purchasing a new construction home is an exciting milestone brimming with anticipation and endless possibilities. While new construction homes are often perceived as pristine and flawless, the decision to have a home inspection remains a prudent step in ensuring your investment is sound and secure. Despite the detailed construction processes of new homes, an independent home inspection offers an additional layer of assurance and insight into the property's condition.

Engaging an independent and qualified home inspector provides you with an impartial evaluation of the property's structure, systems, and components. The inspector can identify deficiencies, oversights, or potential issues requiring attention by conducting a thorough examination.

Even with reputable builders, the possibility of construction defects or errors cannot be entirely ruled out. A home inspector will carefully inspect the home's foundation, framing, electrical systems, plumbing, HVAC, roofing, and other elements to detect any construction issues that warrant correction

Ensuring the new construction home meets local building codes and regulations is paramount for safety and quality standards. A home inspector will assess the property's compliance with building codes, reassuring you that your home is constructed following mandated requirements.

A home inspection instills peace of mind by offering you a comprehensive understanding of the home's condition. Armed with the inspection report, you can address any concerns with the builder, negotiate repairs, or seek necessary modifications before finalizing the purchase, ensuring your home meets your expectations.

Many new construction homes come with warranties from the builder or manufacturer, offering protection against certain defects or issues. A home inspection report can help you identify any problems under warranty coverage, allowing you to address them promptly before the warranty period expires.

Timing of Inspections

Scheduling a home inspection at strategic stages of construction is crucial, ideally before the final walkthrough or closing. This timing allows ample opportunity for necessary repairs, negotiations, or adjustments based on the inspection findings. Engaging a third-party inspector adds an extra layer of objectivity and expertise to the process.

Before the drywall or sheetrock is installed in a new home, a pre-sheet rock inspection is conducted to evaluate the structural, electrical, plumbing, and HVAC systems within the walls. This inspection ensures that all components are correctly installed, meet building codes, and are in good working condition before being concealed by the drywall. Additionally, the pre-sheet rock inspection identifies any potential issues or deficiencies that must be addressed before the walls are closed. By resolving issues at this stage, builders can prevent costly repairs or modifications later in construction. A third-party inspector can provide an unbiased assessment, ensuring the builder meets high standards.

The final walk-through inspection occurs after the drywall has been installed but before the finishing touches are added to the home. This inspection involves a comprehensive walkthrough of the interior spaces to check for defects, imperfections, or incomplete work in the walls, ceilings, and other structural components. It ensures that the drywall installation is high quality, all electrical and plumbing fixtures are correctly placed, and any necessary corrections or adjustments are made before the home is completed. This inspection is crucial in ensuring the interior finishes of the home meet the desired standards of craftsmanship and design. A third-party inspector can offer an impartial evaluation, helping to ensure that all aspects of the home meet your expectations.

Both the pre-sheet rock and final walk-through inspections are essential steps in the construction process of a new home, providing opportunities to catch and address any issues before they become more challenging to rectify. By conducting thorough inspections at key stages of construction with the assistance of a third-party inspector, builders can uphold quality standards, ensure compliance with building codes, and deliver homes that meet homeowners' expectations for safety, durability, and functionality.

When choosing a home inspector, you should prioritize licensed professionals with relevant experience, expertise, and a solid reputation. Request references, inquire about certifications, and make sure the inspector is qualified to conduct a thorough and reliable assessment.

A home inspection for a new construction home is not meant to deter you from purchasing; instead, it aims to provide you with valuable information and insights. By investing in a comprehensive home inspection, you are safeguarding your investment, ensuring the quality and integrity of your home, and beginning your homeownership journey with confidence and clarity.

Homeowners Insurance

Homeowners insurance is crucial for safeguarding your investment in a new construction home. This type of insurance provides financial protection against loss or damage to your home and personal property. Understanding the coverage options and requirements can help ensure you are adequately protected.

Types of Coverage

1. Dwelling Coverage
   - Protects the structure of your home, including walls, roof, and foundation.

2. Personal Property
   - Covers loss or damage to personal items such as furniture, electronics, and clothing.

3. Liability Protection

- Offers protection against legal action for bodily injury or property damage that you or your family members cause to others.

4. Additional Living Expenses
- Covers costs for temporary housing if your home is uninhabitable due to a covered event such as weather conditions.

Shopping for Insurance

Finding the right homeowners insurance involves careful comparison and consideration:
1. Compare Quotes
- Obtain quotes from multiple insurance providers to find the best coverage and rates.
2. Check Reviews
- Research customer reviews and ratings for potential insurers to guarantee reliable service.
3. Ask about Discounts
- Inquire about discounts for new construction homes, security systems, or bundling with other policies (e.g., auto insurance).

Policy Details to Consider

Understanding the details of your policy can help you make informed decisions.
1. Replacement Cost vs. Actual Cash Value
- Choose between replacement cost coverage, which covers the cost to rebuild or repair without depreciation, and actual cash value coverage, which accounts for depreciation. Depreciation is the decrease in a property's value over time

due to wear and tear, outdated features, and external changes.

2. Deductibles

- Understand the deductible amounts and how they affect your premium and out-of-pocket costs in the event of a claim.

3. Exclusions

- Review the policy exclusions to understand what is not covered such as certain natural disasters or specific types of damage.

Maintaining Your Policy

Regular maintenance and review of your policy are essential for ongoing protection:

1. Regular Reviews

- Review your policy annually to ensure it continues to meet your needs as the value of your home and personal belongings change.

2. Update Coverage

- Notify your insurer of any major changes, such as renovations or the addition of valuable items, to keep your coverage up-to-date.

Securing homeowners insurance for your new construction home is critical in protecting your investment. By understanding the types of coverage available, shopping around for the best policy, and maintaining your coverage, you will have peace of mind and financial protection for your new home.

As you start your homeownership journey, understanding the various elements that protect and enhance the value of your investment is crucial. From builder warranties that offer peace of mind to the supportive role of homeowners associations in maintaining community standards, each component plays a vital role in securing your new home. Home inspections provide an extra layer of assurance, ensuring that all aspects of your home meet quality standards and expectations. Meanwhile, homeowners insurance offers financial protection against unforeseen events, providing security for your property and personal belongings.

By familiarizing yourself with these protective measures, you safeguard your investment and ensure a rewarding and confident homeownership experience. This comprehensive approach enables you to navigate potential challenges and make informed decisions that align with your long-term goals. Ultimately, understanding and utilizing these resources set the foundation for a home that truly reflects your aspirations, offering a safe and welcoming environment for years to come.

Chapter 6: Home Financing Options

Mastering the complex world of home financing is a critical step in purchasing a new construction home. This chapter explores the diverse array of financing options available, from Federal Housing Administration (FHA) and conventional loans to specialized Veterans Affairs (VA) and United States Department of Agriculture (USDA) loans, each tailored to different financial profiles and needs. We also examine financial tools such as bridge loans and buydown rates, offering solutions for temporary relief or bridging financing gaps. Emphasis is placed on understanding the importance of managing your debt-to-income ratio, earnest money deposits, and down payments, as these factors significantly influence your mortgage terms and financial strategy. Additionally, we delve into leveraging resources like your 401(k) and understanding the impact of closing costs. The chapter also highlights the potential benefits of down payment and closing cost assistance programs, FICO score models, and builder incentives, all of which can enhance purchasing power and make homeownership more attainable. By the end, you'll be equipped with the knowledge and tools to make informed decisions, ensuring a smooth transition into homeownership while fostering long-term financial stability.

Loan Options

Federal Housing Administration (FHA) Loan: FHA loans are designed to help first-time homebuyers and those with credit scores below the average desirable range. These loans are backed by the Federal Housing Administration, which allows lenders to offer more favorable terms, such as lower down payments and more flexible qualification requirements.

- **Mortgage Insurance Premium** (MIP) is required for FHA loans to protect lenders if borrowers default. It includes:
- **Upfront MIP (UFMIP):** A one-time payment at closing, usually 1.75% of the loan amount.
- **Annual MIP:** A monthly premium added to mortgage payments based on loan amount, term, and loan-to-value (LTV) ratio.
- **Duration**: For LTV > 90%, MIP lasts for the life of the loan. For LTV ≤ 90%, it lasts for 11 years.
- MIP makes FHA loans accessible to those with lower credit scores or smaller down payments but increases overall loan costs.

Conventional Loan: Conventional loans are not insured or guaranteed by the government and typically require higher credit scores and larger down payments than FHA loans. They offer a wide range of terms and rates, making them a popular choice for borrowers with strong credit histories and stable financial backgrounds.

Private Mortgage Insurance (PMI) is required for conventional loans when the down payment is less than 20%. It protects the lender if the borrower defaults. Key points:

- Cost: Typically 0.3% to 1.5% of the loan amount per year.
- Payment: Included in monthly mortgage payments or paid upfront.
- Cancellation: Can usually be canceled when the loan-to-value (LTV) ratio reaches 80%. Lenders must cancel it at 78% LTV.
- Benefit: It allows borrowers to buy a home with a smaller down payment but increases overall mortgage costs.

Veterans Affairs (VA) Loan: VA loans are available to eligible veterans, active-duty service members, and certain members of the National Guard and Reserves. The U.S. Department of Veterans Affairs backs these loans and offers significant benefits, including no down payment, no private mortgage insurance (PMI), and competitive interest rates.

United States Department of Agriculture (USDA) Loan: USDA loans are designed to help low-to-moderate-income individuals and families purchase homes in eligible rural areas. The U.S. Department of Agriculture backs these loans and offer benefits such as no down payment, reduced mortgage insurance costs, and flexible credit requirements.

Bridge Loans: A bridge loan is a helpful financial tool when starting the exciting journey of purchasing a new construction home. It is a short-term loan designed to bridge the financial gap between buying a new home and selling your existing one. Typically lasting from a few months to a year, these loans provide the necessary funds to purchase a new home before your old one is sold.

Buydown Rate

A buydown rate is a mortgage option where the borrower or a third party pays an upfront fee to reduce the interest rate temporarily or permanently. This results in lower monthly payments. There are two main types:

Temporary Buydown: The rate is lowered for the first few years (e.g., a 2-1 buydown lowers the rate by 2% in the first year and 1% in the second year).

Permanent Buydown: The rate is reduced for the entire loan term through a one-time payment.

Benefits include lower initial payments and potential seller incentives. However, it involves upfront costs and may only offer temporary relief.

Fixed Rate

A fixed-rate mortgage is a home loan with an interest rate that remains constant throughout the entire term of the loan. This means your monthly payments stay the same, providing stability and predictability. Typical terms are 15, 20, or 30 years.

That sounds like an exciting project! The debt-to-income (DTI) ratio is an important concept in real estate, especially for potential homebuyers. Lenders often use it to assess a borrower's ability to manage monthly payments and repay debts.

Debt-to-Income (DTI) Ratio

When you're ready to buy a home, one of the key financial metrics lenders will consider is your Debt-to-Income (DTI) ratio. This ratio measures your ability to manage monthly payments and repay debts. It's expressed as a percentage and is calculated by dividing your total monthly debt payments by your gross monthly income.

Why is DTI Important?

Lenders use the DTI ratio to gauge the risk of lending you money. A lower DTI ratio indicates a good balance between debt and income, which suggests you're less likely to default on your mortgage. Conversely, a higher DTI ratio might signal that you have too much debt relative to your income, making you a riskier borrower.

How to Calculate Your DTI Ratio

1. Add Up Your Monthly Debts: This includes all your recurring monthly expenses such as:
   - Mortgage or rent payments
   - Credit card payments
   - Auto loans
   - Student loans
   - Any other personal loans

2. Determine Your Gross Monthly Income: Before taxes and other deductions, this is your income. Include:
   - Salary
   - Wages
   - Bonuses
   - Commissions

- Any other regular income sources

3. Calculate the Ratio: Divide your total monthly debt payments by your gross monthly income and multiply by 100 to get a percentage.

Ideal DTI Ratios

Most lenders prefer a DTI ratio of 43% or less, with no more than 28% of that debt going towards your mortgage. However, some lenders may accept higher ratios, especially if you have a strong credit score or other compensating factors.

Tips for Managing Your DTI Ratio

- Pay Down Debt: Focus on reducing high-interest debts first.
- Increase Income: Consider ways to boost your income, such as a side job or freelance work.
- Avoid New Debt: Minimize taking on new debts before applying for a mortgage.
- Budget Wisely: Keep a close eye on your spending and prioritize essential expenses.
Understanding and managing your DTI ratio can make a significant difference in your ability to secure a mortgage and find your dream home.

Earnest Money Deposit

An earnest money deposit, or good faith deposit, is a sum a buyer provides to a seller to demonstrate their intent to purchase a property. This deposit is typically made shortly after the offer to purchase is accepted and is held in escrow until the closing of the real estate transaction. The earnest money deposit shows that the buyer is committed to the sale and is willing to proceed with the purchasing process. If the sale goes through, the earnest money deposit is typically applied toward the down payment or closing costs. If the sale falls through for reasons specified in the contract, the earnest money deposit may be returned to the buyer.

Down Payment

A down payment is an upfront payment made by a homebuyer towards the purchase price of a property. It represents a portion of the total cost and is typically expressed as a percentage of the purchase price. For example, a 20% down payment on a $300,000 home would amount to $60,000. The down payment reduces the amount of money that needs to be financed through a mortgage, lowering the loan amount and potentially the monthly mortgage payments. The size of the down payment can also influence the terms of the loan, including interest rates and the requirement for private mortgage insurance (PMI). Making a larger down payment can benefit buyers by reducing their overall debt and demonstrating financial stability to lenders.

Leveraging Your 401(k) for Homeownership

Using your 401(k) to purchase a new construction home can be a viable option for those looking to bridge the gap in down payments or cover other upfront costs. The most common methods include taking a 401(k) loan or making a hardship withdrawal. A 401(k) loan allows you to borrow against your retirement savings, typically up to 50% of the vested balance or $50,000, whichever is less. The loan must be repaid with interest, usually within five years, to avoid penalties and taxes. On the other hand, a hardship withdrawal enables you to withdraw funds without the obligation of repayment. Still, it has significant tax implications and potential early withdrawal penalties if you're under 59½. While these options can provide immediate financial relief, it's crucial to consider the long-term impact on your retirement savings and consult with a financial advisor to ensure this strategy aligns with your overall financial goals.

Closing Costs

Closing costs are the fees and expenses that homebuyers and sellers must pay at the finalization of a real estate transaction, commonly called the closing or settlement. These costs typically include various administrative, legal, and financial fees for purchasing a home. Standard closing costs for buyers may include loan origination fees, appraisal fees, title insurance, escrow or settlement fees, property taxes, homeowner's insurance, and recording fees. The total closing costs can range from 2% to 5% of the home's purchase price, depending on the specifics of the transaction and the location of the property. Buyers need to budget for these costs in addition to the down payment, as they are due at the time of closing and are necessary to complete the purchase of the home.

Down Payment Assistance

Down payment assistance (DPA) refers to programs designed to help homebuyers cover a portion or all of the down payment required to purchase a home. These programs can also assist with closing costs. Down payment assistance can come in various forms, including grants, low —or no-interest loans, deferred payment loans, or forgivable loans. Federal, state, or local government agencies, nonprofit organizations, and some private lenders often offer these programs.

Eligibility for down payment assistance typically depends on factors such as the buyer's income, credit score, and home purchase price. Some programs specifically target first-time homebuyers, veterans, or individuals purchasing homes in certain geographic areas. The benefits of utilizing down payment assistance include making homeownership more accessible, reducing the money a buyer needs to save upfront, and potentially lowering monthly mortgage payments.

To apply for down payment assistance, buyers usually must provide documentation of their income, assets, and other financial details to demonstrate eligibility. Understanding and leveraging these programs can significantly ease the financial burden of purchasing a home and make achieving homeownership a more attainable goal.

Closing Cost Assistance

Closing cost assistance refers to programs and incentives designed to help homebuyers cover the fees and expenses due at the finalization of a real estate transaction, known as the closing or settlement. These costs include loan origination fees, appraisal fees, title insurance, escrow or settlement fees, property taxes, homeowner's insurance, and recording fees. Closing cost assistance can come in several forms, such as grants, low- or no-interest loans, or credits from the seller or lender.

These programs are often offered by federal, state, or local government agencies, nonprofit organizations, and sometimes by private lenders. Eligibility for closing cost assistance typically depends on factors such as the buyer's income, credit score, and home purchase price. Some programs are tailored to first-time homebuyers, veterans, or buyers purchasing homes in specific geographic areas.

The benefits and application process of closing cost assistance are similar to the down payment assistance program process.

Understanding Your Credit Score

Your credit score plays a crucial role in your ability to secure a mortgage and can significantly affect the terms and interest rates offered. A higher credit score generally means better mortgage terms and lower interest rates.

Credit Score Ranges

The next page shows a general guide to credit score ranges and what they typically mean for home buyers:

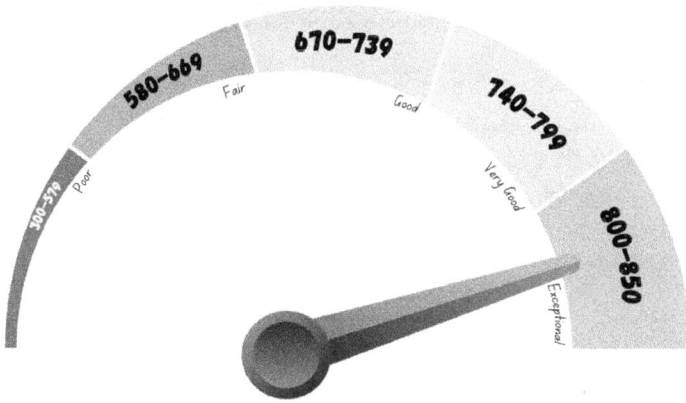

Credit Score Range	Rating	Impact on Mortgage Options
800-850	Exceptional	Excellent interest rates and terms
740-799	Very Good	Very good interest rates and terms
670-739	Good	Good interest rates and terms
580-669	Fair	Higher interest rates, limited options
300-579	Poor	Very high interest rates may need to improve score before buying

Tips for Improving Your Credit Score

Understanding your credit score and how it impacts your mortgage options is an important step in the home buying process. Use the chart above as a quick reference to gauge where you stand and take steps to improve your score if necessary.

TIPS TO IMPROVE YOUR CREDIT SCORE

Pay Bills on Time

Consistently paying your bills on time can have a positive impact on your credit score.

Reduce Debt

Lowering your credit card balances and overall debt can improve your score.

Check for Errors

Regularly check your credit report for errors and dispute inaccuracies.

Limit New Credit Inquiries

Avoid applying for new credit in the months leading up to your mortgage application.

FICO Score Models

When it comes to securing a mortgage, lenders rely on specific FICO score models to evaluate the creditworthiness of potential borrowers. The three primary FICO score models used in mortgage lending are FICO Score 2, FICO Score 4, and FICO Score 5. FICO Score 2, also known as the Experian/Fair Isaac Risk Model v2, is utilized by Experian for assessing mortgage applications. FICO Score 4, referred to as the TransUnion/FICO Risk Score 04, is employed by TransUnion for mortgage-related credit evaluations. Lastly, FICO Score 5, or the Equifax Beacon 5.0 Score, is used by Equifax in mortgage lending scenarios. These models are part of an older generation of FICO scores chosen for their established reliability in predicting mortgage default risk. They play a crucial role in the underwriting process for conventional and government-backed mortgages, helping lenders make informed decisions about a borrower's ability to repay a home loan.

Builder Incentives

When purchasing a new construction home, you must be aware of builder incentives that can enhance your buying experience. Builder incentives are special offers or discounts to attract buyers and expedite the sale of new homes. These incentives can include covering closing costs, offering free upgrades, such as premium countertops or flooring, and financing deals with lower interest rates. Buyers can secure a better overall deal on their new home by taking advantage of these incentives, making the dream of owning a new home even more attainable. Always inquire about available builder incentives and negotiate effectively to maximize the benefits in your favor.

"Avoid opening new lines of credit while in a real estate transaction. Lenders will re-evaluate your credit before finalizing the mortgage, and any new credit inquiries or accounts could negatively impact your loan approval."

Taxes and Equity

Purchasing a new construction home is an exciting venture, but it also involves various financial considerations, with property taxes being among the most significant. Property taxes, special assessments, and other municipal levies contribute to the overall cost of homeownership. Understanding these financial obligations is crucial for making informed decisions and effectively managing your responsibilities. Additionally, recognizing opportunities for building equity in your new home can offer long-term financial benefits and stability. This section will guide you through property taxes, special assessments, Municipal Utility District (MUD) and Planned Unit Development (PUD) taxes, tax incentives, and strategies for building equity in your new construction home.

Property Taxes

One of the primary forms of taxation for homeowners is property taxes, which are levied based on the property's assessed value and play a crucial role in funding local services and infrastructure. Property tax rates can vary significantly across different communities, even within the same jurisdiction, impacting the overall cost of homeownership and the quality of services available.

Special Assessments

In addition to property taxes, new communities may impose special assessments to cover the costs of specific improvements or services benefiting residents, such as road maintenance, landscaping, or community amenities. Understanding the presence and scope of special assessments in a community is essential for evaluating the overall financial obligations associated with homeownership.

Municipal Utility District Taxes

A Municipal Utility District (MUD) is a special-purpose district or entity created by a local government to provide specific services, such as water, sewage, and drainage, to residents of a designated area. MUD taxes are assessments levied by the district to fund the infrastructure and services it provides. These taxes are typically included in property tax bills and are used to cover the costs of maintaining and operating the utilities and services within the district.

Planned Unit Development Taxes

A Planned Unit Development (PUD) is a type of development project in which a mix of residential, commercial, and recreational properties are planned and built as a single entity. PUD taxes refer to any property taxes or assessments associated with living in or owning property within a PUD. These taxes may vary depending on the amenities and services provided within the development such as parks, common areas, or shared facilities.

MUD and PUD taxes support the infrastructure, services, and amenities within the designated district or development. Property owners within these areas are typically responsible for paying these taxes to help the community's ongoing maintenance and operation.

Tax Incentives or Abatements

Some new communities may offer tax incentives or discounts to attract homeowners and promote development. These incentives can range from reduced property tax rates to temporary tax breaks, offering financial advantages to residents. Exploring the availability of tax incentives or abatements in a community can provide valuable insights into potential savings and long-term affordability.

Homestead Exemptions

Homestead exemptions serve as tax benefits for homeowners who use their property as their primary residence, offering relief from the property tax burden. Understanding the availability and extent of homestead exemptions in a jurisdiction can help homeowners maximize their tax savings and manage their financial responsibilities effectively.

Tax Exemptions

Understanding tax exemptions available to homeowners, especially for specific demographics like seniors and veterans, is essential for maximizing savings and financial resources. For instance, individuals over 65 may qualify for tax exemptions or reductions on property taxes based on their age and income level. Similarly, 100% disabled veterans are often eligible for significant property tax exemptions as a gesture of recognition and support for their service and sacrifice. Additionally, veterans with disabilities below 100% may qualify for property tax exemptions or reductions based on their level of disability and service-related conditions.

Equity in New Construction Homes

Building equity in a new construction home offers a unique opportunity to grow your financial investment from the ground up. Equity is the difference between your home's market value and the remaining balance on your mortgage. When you purchase a new construction home, you start building equity as soon as you make your down payment and continue with each mortgage payment. Additionally, new homes are often appreciated due to modern amenities, energy efficiency, and desirable locations, increasing your equity over time. Unlike older homes that may require costly repairs and updates, new construction homes typically come with warranties and lower maintenance costs, enabling you to preserve and grow your equity more effectively. Understanding how to build and leverage equity in your new home can provide long-term financial benefits, including the potential for home equity loans or lines of credit for future investments or major expenses.

Appreciation

A cornerstone of equity growth appreciation is the gradual increase in the market value of your new construction home over time. Influenced by factors such as market dynamics, location desirability, and demand trends, appreciation augments your equity stake in the property. Upon future resale, the variance between the sale price and the original purchase price contributes to expanding your equity base, reflecting the enduring value of your home investment.

Navigating the various tax obligations and opportunities for building equity in a new construction home can be complex. Still, with the proper knowledge and planning, you can make informed decisions that support your financial goals. You can better anticipate and manage your financial responsibilities by understanding property taxes, special assessments, MUD and PUD taxes, tax incentives, and exemptions. Additionally, focusing on building equity in your new home will provide long-term financial stability and open doors to future opportunities. With this knowledge, you'll be well-prepared to make the most of your new construction home investment.

As we conclude Chapter 6 on home financing options, you now possess a comprehensive understanding of the various financial tools and considerations involved in purchasing a new construction home. From exploring different loan types —such as FHA, conventional, VA, and USDA loans—to understanding the elements of bridge loans and buydown rates, you've gained insights into how each option can align with your unique financial circumstances and goals. Additionally, we've analyzed the importance of managing your debt-to-income ratio, the role of earnest money deposits, and the impact of down payments on your mortgage terms.

Your journey also touched upon leveraging your 401(k) and other financial resources, understanding and budgeting for closing costs, and exploring down payment and closing cost assistance programs. Furthermore, we've highlighted the critical role of FICO scores and credit management in securing favorable mortgage terms and the potential benefits of builder incentives.

Finally, we examined the implications of taxes and equity, emphasizing the importance of understanding property taxes, special assessments, and opportunities for building and leveraging equity in your new home. Armed with this knowledge, you are now better equipped to navigate the complex financial landscape of homeownership. By making informed decisions and effectively managing your financial resources, you can achieve your dream of owning a new construction home while ensuring long-term financial stability and growth.

What You Should Have Learned

By reading *Home Sweet New Home*, you've gained valuable insights into the home buying process, from understanding market trends and financing options to knowing the difference between builders and negotiating deals. You now have a solid grasp of identifying your needs and preferences, navigating the complexities of real estate transactions, and making informed decisions to secure your dream home. More importantly, you've learned how to avoid common pitfalls and maximize the value of your investment.

With this knowledge, it's time to put theory into practice. Create a detailed checklist of your home buying criteria, including location, budget, non-negotiable features, and future growth potential. Research neighborhoods to refine your preferences further. Engage with a real estate agent who can offer expert guidance tailored to your needs.

Take the next step towards your new home by setting a concrete deadline. Contact a real estate agent within 30-60 days to discuss your home buying goals. Next, identify three potential builders in your area and research their offerings thoroughly. Document your findings, noting what you liked and disliked about each builder's offerings, approach, and quality of work. Use this information to refine your search criteria and make well-informed decisions. This proactive approach will boost your confidence and bring you closer to finding your perfect home.

Congratulations on your new home!

Latosca Asberry, Realtor & Writer

Latosca Asberry is a dedicated real estate agent and writer based in Dallas. With a diverse background in banking, retail, and the medical field, she brings a wealth of experience in accounts receivable and retail sales to her real estate career. Latosca's love for writing from the heart is a personal pursuit that beautifully complements her ventures in real estate.

Her educational journey at Tarrant County College and Dallas Baptist University has shaped her multifaceted career, providing her with a solid foundation for success.

Outside of her professional life, Latosca enjoys practicing yoga and exploring the trails on her bike—activities that help her maintain balance and inspire her creativity. She believes in authenticity and continuous self-improvement, guiding her approach to life and work with integrity and determination.

Currently, Latosca is immersed in her writing passion projects and anticipates the opportunity to share her books with the world. Connect with her on social media to learn more about her inspiring journey and future endeavors.